Early American
COOKING

Recipes from Western Historic Sites

COMPILED AND EDITED BY
EVELYN L. BEILENSON

 PETER PAUPER PRESS, INC. WHITE PLAINS · NEW YORK

A PETER
PAUPER
PRESS
BOOK

For John, Laurence, Suzanne

ISBN 0-88088-915-2
Library of Congress Catalog No. 86-060105
Printed in the United States of America
Designed & Decorated by J.E. O'Neill
Interior Decorations by Ming Louie

CONTENTS

4

EARLY AMERICAN COOKING

*Recipes
from Western
Historic Sites*

EXPLORERS, PROSPECTORS, COWBOYS AND SETTLERS who pushed West in the 19th Century faced constant challenges as they struggled to survive, establish roots, and prosper. The animals they hunted, the crops they planted, and the food they ate depended on the local area, while how they cooked was most often a reflection of their cultures.

The Native Americans (Indians) taught the newcomers valuable survival techniques. Their "iron ration" of pemmican and jerky provided the white man with a nutritious staple on the trail and during the long hard winters.

Early American Cooking: Recipes from Western Historic Sites introduces the reader to twenty of the great historic sites from the Mississippi to the Pacific and to the cuisine served at or near these sites, both traditionally and at the present time.

The recipes in italics are original recipes dating back at least 100 years. All other recipes are modern adaptations of old dishes. Today's cook should approach the original recipes with great caution, however, since ingredients and cooking methods were different from their modern-day equivalents.

Personnel at the historic sites generously provided information about their respective sites and donated original recipes. Modern recipes were in most cases compiled by the editor, the author of a number of Peter Pauper Press cookbooks.

It is the editor's wish that the reader will enjoy his or her travels to these historic western sites and will gain a new admiration and understanding of America's pioneers by preparing and savoring the foods they ate. Westward Ho!

E.L.B.

THE ALAMO

THE ALAMO in San Antonio, Texas stands as a reminder of the 183 men who in March, 1836 gave their lives defending their country against Santa Anna's 1,800-man Mexican army.

John W. Smith was one of the last messengers dispatched from the Alamo before its fall on March 6, 1836. Colonel William Barret Travis, the Alamo commander, possibly wanted to get Smith, a young man with a pregnant wife, out of the fort before its final demise. The little girl born to Smith and his wife a few months later grew up and married William G. Tobin, the inventor of canned chili.

Chili con carne, or chili, is the official food of Texas, and some experts claim that San Antonio is the birthplace of the dish. Originally, chili con carne probably included only meat and red chilis and perhaps comino, oregano and garlic. No one really knows the history of chili, but it was without question served in San Antonio as early as the 1820's.

In 1898 William Gebhardt, who invented "chili powder," moved his factory to San Antonio and shortly thereafter printed what is believed to be the first Mexican cookbook published in this country. The following old recipe for chili comes from that book.

Gebhardt's Eagle (Standard)
Chili Con Carne

Cut two pounds of beef into one-half inch squares, add about two ounces chopped tallow, then salt it. Use a high pot (granite-ware is best), heat in this pot two tablespoonsful of lard; add to this a small-sized chopped onion; when the onion is about half done, add the meat; stir well until the meat is separated and white, then let steam or parboil (with cover off) over a rather hot fire, stirring frequently until the juice of the meat is boiled down, and when it starts to fry add about one and one-half pints of hot water, three tablespoonsful of Gebhardt's Eagle Chili Powder and a few buttons of chopped garlic; stir well and let simmer until meat is tender.

The Chili Lover's Prayer

Lord, God, you know us old cowhands is forgetful. Sometimes, I can't even recollect what happened yesterday. We is forgetful. We just know daylight from dark, summer, fall, winter, and spring. But I sure hope we don't never forget to thank you before we eat a mess of good chili.

We don't know why, in your wisdom, you been so doggone good to us. The heathen Chinese don't have no chili, never. The Frenchmen is left out. The Russians don't know no more about chili than a hog knows about a sidesaddle. Even the Mexicans don't get a good wiff of chili unless they live around here.

Chili-eaters is some of your chosen people, Lord. We don't know why you're so doggone good to us. But, Lord God, don't never think we ain't grateful for this chili we are about to eat. Amen.

Anonymous

CHILI-CON-CARNE

2   pounds stew meat, cut in 1/2″ cubes (not ground)
1   large yellow onion, cut up
1   head garlic (10-12 cloves), minced
3-5 tablespoons chili powder
2   tablespoons ground comino
1   teaspoon salt
½   teaspoon black pepper
⅔   large can of tomato juice
⅓   large can of water

Brown meat in cast iron skillet or pot. Add seasonings, onion and garlic. Mix well. Add water and tomato juice and bring to boil. Lower heat and simmer for two hours, stirring every 5 minutes. Cool, refrigerate, let set overnight. Reheat and serve with pinto beans and warmed corn tortillas. May be served with fresh, finely chopped onion, if desired. While cooking, be sure to stir about every 5-10 minutes, in order not to burn or scorch the chili. This recipe can be made in crock-pot or microwave successfully by lessening the amount of water and tomato juice added in the beginning since in a crock-pot or microwave the water does not evaporate to the extent it does on the stove. Chili-con-carne reheats very well in the microwave, and the crock-pot is an ideal way to serve the dish, particularly for buffet service.

William Elton Green

THE AMANA COLONIES

THE AMANA (IOWA) COLONIES were founded in
the mid-19th Century by members of a
German Lutheran separatist group, the
Inspirationists. Facing persecution in Germany,
they came to America in the 1840's and settled
near Buffalo, New York. In 1854, they moved on
to fertile farmland in the Iowa River Valley,
built six small villages and purchased the
Village of Homestead to gain access to the
railroad.

Until the "Great Change" of 1932 the
Colonists had individual homes but cooked
and dined in communal fashion. Men and
women ate at separate tables, and meals were
served four or five times a day. Residents used
their "purchase books" when they needed
groceries, yard goods, shoes, quilts or toys. In
1932 common property was dissolved and
distributed as corporate stock.

Amana buildings are utilitarian and
picturesque; the Colonies look very different
from other Iowa towns. Church services occur
without an organ or instrumental music, and
the dead are buried in rows as they die,
generally not in family plots.

"Amana" means "remain faithful" and this
the Colonists have done not only in their
religion and cooperative spirit but in their
cooking as well. The recipes that follow are
traditional German recipes from Amana.

POTATO PANCAKES

6 large potatoes, peeled and finely grated
4 eggs, beaten
2 tablespoons flour
1 teaspoon salt
  Dash of pepper
½ cup vegetable oil

Place grated potato pulp in a cheese-cloth and press out all excess water. Put potatoes into a mixing bowl, add remaining ingredients except oil, and mix well. Heat oil in skillet. Drop mixture by tablespoon into hot oil and smooth into patties. Fry until both sides are golden brown. Serve with applesauce.

POTATO SOUP

4 slices lean bacon, diced
6 leeks, thinly sliced
¼ cup onion, chopped
2 tablespoons flour
4 cups chicken broth
3 large potatoes, thinly sliced
2 egg yolks, beaten
1 cup sour cream
3 tablespoons parsley, chopped

Saute bacon in a deep saucepan for 5 minutes. Add leeks and onions and saute for 5 minutes. Stir in flour. Slowly add the chicken broth, stirring constantly. Add potatoes and simmer for 1 hour. Mix in blender or food processor until creamy. Combine egg yolks and sour cream. Add to soup. Simmer for 10 minutes, stirring constantly. Garnish with fresh chopped parsley. Makes about 2 quarts.

Honey Cookies

2 cups honey
1 tablespoon baking soda
2 tablespoons butter
½ cup granulated sugar
½ cup brown sugar
3 eggs, beaten
5 to 6 cups flour

Let honey come to a boil. Take off heat. Add soda. Melt butter in honey and soda. Cool to lukewarm. Mix in sugar, eggs and flour and chill overnight. Roll on lightly floured board to ⅛ inch thickness and cut with floured cookie cutter. Bake on greased baking sheet at 325 degrees for 8 to 10 minutes or until cookies appear to be done. Dust with confectioners' sugar.

Chocolate Cookies

1½ cups butter
4 cups sugar
8 eggs
5–6 cups flour
3 teaspoons baking powder
1½ cups cocoa

With an electric mixer blend butter, sugar and eggs. Blend in flour, baking powder and cocoa. Drop mixture by the teaspoon on lightly greased cookie sheet. Bake in 325 degree oven for 8–10 minutes.

Boot Hill Museum

The Old West comes alive at the Boot Hill Museum in downtown Dodge City, Kansas, where Fort Dodge was established in 1865.

Starting in 1876, Longhorn cattle from Texas were driven up the Chisholm Trail and the Western Trail to the Santa Fe Railway's loading pens in Dodge City. On the long drive from Texas to Kansas 1500 to 3000 head of cattle were accompanied by 10 to 15 cowboys, a wrangler for the horses, a trail boss and a cook.

The average age of a cowboy was 24 and about one of three was either Mexican or black. Cowboys led a very hard life. They sometimes went hungry, got wet and cold, got "cussed" by the boss, and were even invaded by body lice.

Meals were eaten from the chuckwagon. Breakfast was at daybreak, lunch at 11:00 A.M. and dinner at dark. Meals on the trail, although filling, often lacked nutritional value. A cowboy's diet consisted mostly of biscuits, bacon, beef, beans, dried prunes or apples, and coffee.

Typical cowboy's dishes, from which variations were created on the trail, are presented on the following pages.

17

Sonofabitch Stew was referred to in polite company by cowboys as Sonofagun Stew

SONOFABITCH STEW

2 pounds lean beef
Half a calf heart
1½ pounds calf liver
1 set sweetbreads
1 set brains
1 set marrow gut
Salt, pepper to taste
Louisiana hot sauce

Kill off a young steer. Cut up beef, liver and heart into 1-inch cubes; slice the marrow gut into small rings. Place in a Dutch oven or deep casserole. Cover meat with water and simmer for 2 to 3 hours. Add salt, pepper and hot sauce to taste. Take sweetbreads and brains and cut into small pieces. Add to stew. Simmer another hour, never boiling.

SOURDOUGH STARTER

2 cups lukewarm potato water
2 cups flour
1 tablespoon sugar

First make potato water by cutting up 2 medium-sized potatoes into cubes, and boil in 3 cups of water until tender. Remove the potatoes and measure out 2 cups of remaining liquid. Mix the potato water, flour and sugar into a smooth paste. Set in a warm place until starter mixture rises to double its original size.

SOURDOUGH BISCUITS

1   cup sourdough starter
1   teaspoon each of salt, sugar, and baking soda
1   tablespoon shortening
3 to 4   cups sifted flour

Place flour in a bowl, make a well in the center and add sourdough starter (above). Stir in salt, soda and sugar, and add shortening. Gradually mix in enough flour to make a stiff dough. Pinch off dough for one biscuit at a time; form a ball and roll it in melted shortening. Crowd the biscuits in a round 8-inch cake pan and allow to rise in a warm place for 20 to 30 minutes before baking. Bake at 425 degrees until done.

VINEGAR PIE

1   cup sugar
2   tablespoons flour
1   cup cold water
4   eggs, beaten
5   tablespoons vinegar
2½   tablespoons butter

Combine sugar and flour. Add the rest of the ingredients and place in a saucepan. Cook until thick and pour into a prepared pie crust. Bake in a 375 degree oven until the crust is brown.

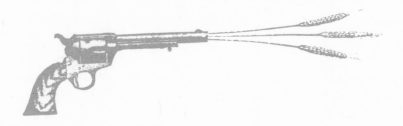

BRIGHAM YOUNG'S HOUSE

THE BEEHIVE HOUSE in Salt Lake City, Utah was the home of Brigham Young, pioneer, President of the Church of Jesus Christ of Latter-day Saints (Mormons) and Governor of the Territory of Deseret (Utah).

Erected in 1854, the House was designed to meet the varied needs of Brigham Young; it served both as the official residence of the Mormon leader as well as his family home and family store. The House derived its name from the beehive-shaped cupola (the beehive being the traditional symbol of industry) that stood atop the two-story-and-attic main portion of the house.

Lucy Decker Young, one of Brigham Young's 27 wives, served as hostess and overseer of the house. Some of Young's other wives lived next door in the Lion House or in homes that he deeded to them. In all, Young had 56 children, 31 daughters and 25 sons.

The following recipe belonged to Emily Dow Partridge Young, wife of Brigham Young. Because there was not a great variety of foods, when something was made it was generally made in large quantity, and was doubled in size. You may double the recipe or cut it in half, and you will find the doughnuts are as tender and crisp and delicious as anything made out of a modern cookbook. Nutmeg, incidentally, was a chief spice in the early days and was grated tediously by hand over tiny metal nutmeg graters.

BRIGHAM'S BUTTERMILK DOUGHNUTS

2 cups buttermilk
2 large eggs, beaten
1 cup sugar
5 cups sifted flour
1 teaspoon baking powder
1 teaspoon salt
1 teaspoon grated nutmeg
¼ cup melted butter or shortening

Combine buttermilk, eggs, and sugar, and blend well. Beat in sifted dry ingredients, then stir in melted butter. Roll or pat dough on floured board about ¼ inch thick and cut with 2½-inch doughnut cutter. Fry in hot fat (at 375 degrees) until golden brown on both sides. Drain and sprinkle with sugar, if desired. Makes 2 dozen doughnuts.

RICE PUDDING

2 cups cooked rice
2 cups milk
1 small can (5⅓ ounces) evaporated milk
½ cup raisins
1 tablespoon cornstarch
¼ teaspoon salt
½ cup plus 2 tablespoons sugar
2 eggs slightly beaten
⅛ teaspoon nutmeg
⅛ teaspoon cinnamon
1 teaspoon vanilla

In a small saucepan, scald the milks together. Measure raisins into a strainer and set over boiling water just long enough to plump them. In a heavy 2- or 3-quart saucepan combine cornstarch, salt, and sugar, and blend well. Stir in hot milk mixture, stirring constantly over medium heat until thick and smooth. Add rice; reheat to a full boil. Remove from heat. Pour a little of the hot mixture into beaten eggs while stirring rapidly. Return egg mixture to hot milk and rice and stir until thickened (only a minute or two). Remove from heat. Stir in raisins, spices and vanilla. Chill. Makes eight ½-cup servings.

CABRILLO NATIONAL MONUMENT

THE CABRILLO NATIONAL MONUMENT in San Diego, California marks the location of the landing in 1542 of Juan Rodriguez Cabrillo, the first European to explore what is now America's West Coast.

At the Park, visitors can visit one of the earliest U.S. Government lighthouses on the Pacific Coast, at Point Loma.

On November 15, 1855 the original lighthouse keeper first lit the lamp which was for 36 years to welcome sailors, prospectors, settlers and merchants to the West Coast.

Less welcoming were the rough conditions and isolation under which the lighthouse keepers, and in some cases their families, lived. Growing one's own food was out of the question.

The Lighthouse Board provided isolated lighthouses such as Point Loma with 200 pounds of pork, 100 pounds of beef, two barrels of flour, 50 pounds of rice, 50 pounds of sugar, 24 pounds of coffee, 10 gallons of beans or peas, four gallons of vinegar and two barrels of potatoes a year. With these basic provisions plus some added ingredients the imaginative keeper or wife might well have made one of these recipes from the 1800's when the lighthouse was in use.

Irish Soda Bread

    2 cups flour
1½ teaspoons baking powder
¼ teaspoon baking soda
1 or 2 tablespoons sugar
½ cup buttermilk
1 tablespoon oil
½ teaspoon salt

Mix all ingredients together, turn out on floured board and knead for two minutes, shape into 8″ diameter loaf. Place on greased baking sheet, cut X on top with sharp knife. Bake at 350 degrees for about 40 minutes. One half cup of raisins or one tablespoon caraway seeds or both can be added. If desired, top with butter when first taken from oven. Cool on rack.

Natal Plum Jam

    6 cups Natal Plums
½ cup water
5 or 6 cups sugar
½ bottle of Certo

Wash 6 cups Natal Plums and cut into halves or quarters, depending on size. Scoop out seeds with a spoon. Boil plums for 5 minutes with ½ cup water. Add about 5 or 6 cups sugar, bring to full boil again for another minute, stirring constantly. Remove from heat, and as soon as mixture stops boiling, add ½ bottle of Certo and stir for 5 minutes more. Pour into sterilized glasses and cover with paraffin.

BREAD AND BUTTER PICKLES

3 cucumbers sliced paper thin with skin (well washed
   to remove paraffin used on purchased cucumbers)
2 medium onions, sliced thin, separated into rings
½ green pepper, cut into thin strips
2 tablespoons salt
⅝ cup sugar (½ + 2 tablespoons)
⅝ cup cider vinegar
¼ teaspoon ground mustard
⅛ teaspoon ground tumeric
4 whole cloves

Place vegetables in layers, sprinkle with salt. Place a
layer of ice cubes on top, then a plate and then a
weight. Let stand 3 hours, drain. Bring sugar, cider
vinegar, mustard, tumeric and cloves to boil in
stainless steel pan, add drained vegetables, cook 5
minutes. Place in sterilized jars or in refrigerator.
Ready in 5 days.

CUSTER BATTLEFIELD
NATIONAL MONUMENT

CUSTER BATTLEFIELD NATIONAL MONUMENT in Montana commemorates one of the final armed efforts of the Sioux and Cheyenne to preserve their ancestral way of life.

Here in the valley of Little Bighorn River in June, 1876 Lt. Col. George Armstrong Custer and 260 soldiers and attached personnel of the U.S. Army made their "last stand" against several thousand warriors. Although the Indians won the battle, they subsequently lost the war in that they were forced to return to the reservation and give up their nomadic way of life.

During their travels (such as on war parties, scouting parties and hunting parties), Plains Indians subsisted on a food called pemmican. It contained practically everything the body needed for proper nutrition, and was also very light to carry. When making pemmican back in the buffalo days Indians did not have sugar or margarine as they do today. In place of these ingredients they used wild plants which were sweet, and fat from the buffalo.

PEMMICAN

1 pound chokecherries
1 round steak or deer meat, sliced into thin strips
1-1½ quarts water
2 cubes margarine per pound of meat
   Sugar to taste

Allow a day to dry chokecherries and meat in the following way:

Grind fresh berries, seeds and all. Dry in hamburger-size patties in the sun. When very dry break patties into bits and place in a pot of water. Boil until chokecherries are soft. Drain water from pot and mash chokecherries. Dry meat in the sun and turn occasionally until meat is very dark and dry. Meat will turn almost a blackish color. DO NOT hang meat on wire. Hang meat over wooden object or stick. When meat is dry it will be crispy and break easily. Place strips of meat on a cookie sheet and bake at about 300 degrees turning strips every 2 minutes until meat smells as if it is baked (you have to go by aroma and not time). Take meat out of the oven and break or crumble. Grind in a meat grinder. Meat will now be a light tan color and ready to mix with cherries. Melt margarine. Add margarine to meat and cherry mixture. Add sugar to taste. Form mixture into balls about the size of small baseballs and refrigerate. Best to eat when cooled for a day or so.

Flour as we know it today did not exist for the Plains Indians. The pulp matter from some roots was very similar to powder and was used as flour. The following bread was made by Plains Indians after the introduction of regular flour when traders came amongst them in the mid-1770's.

FIRESIDE BREAD OR PAN BREAD

2 cups of sifted flour
2 teaspoons baking powder
½ teaspoon salt
½ cup of shortening
¾ cup fresh or canned milk

Knead all ingredients to mix them. When rolling out dough, you should make it about ¼ inch thick, no more. Roll out dough into size of your frying pan. Slightly grease frying pan before placing bread in it. If camping, prop your frying pan against fire; if at home, put on medium heat or flame. Turn over the bread several times until cooked. This bread is similar to a thick tortilla-type bread and is delicious with butter, honey, or syrup.

INDIAN PUDDING

1 pound wild blueberries or chokeberries
4 cups water
½ cup flour
1 cup sugar

Boil berries in water. Drain juice and set aside. Mash berries and mix with ½ cup flour. Combine sugar and juice and mix together with berries. Stir. If some lumps are in the pudding add a little more water. Boil slowly, stirring constantly until thick. Cool and serve.

FORT DAVIS NATIONAL HISTORIC SITE

F ORT DAVIS, located on the northern edge of
the town of Fort Davis, Texas, was
established in 1854 as a post on the San
Antonio-El Paso road to protect settlers who
were emigrating west. At that time, there were
very few permanent settlers in the area. For
the most part West Texas was a lonely stretch
of country through which Indians from the
Oklahoma and New Mexico territories
traversed to raid villages in Northern Mexico.

Many of the people who first settled this
area of western Texas were of Mexican
ancestry so that recipes of the late 19th
Century were a blend of both Mexican and
American traditions.

In this part of the country, although sheep
were (and still are) raised, very little lamb was
eaten. Bar-be-ques (and the term referred to
the whole meal rather than just the meat)
centered around beef, antelope, or goat meat.
The meat was hung on a rack or spit over red
oak or mesquite wood coals and cooked for
several hours. The old timers say the secret of
good bar-be-que meat is the sauce which is
applied to the meat after cooking. One old
recipe for bar-be-que sauce is as follows:

Bar-be-que Sauce

1 cup catsup or tomato sauce
2 teaspoons chili powder
$1/3$ cup Worcestershire sauce
2 tablespoons lemon juice
2 teaspoons salt
$1/4$ cup chopped onion
1 tablespoon brown sugar
2 garlic cloves, minced
2 cups water
2 tablespoons butter

Combine all ingredients and bring to a boil.

Many of the old recipes of the area are Mexican in origin. One in particular is still a favorite. It is for asaderos--a cheese made from a local weed.

Asaderos

$1/2$ gallon raw sweet milk
1 gallon raw sour milk
$1/2$ cup hot water
8 medium trompillos (yellow are best)

Mix both milks together and warm on a very low burner or by settling in a warm place. Let it clabber. In the meantime, mash the trompillos in the hot water and strain the juice into the clabbering milk. Stir and allow the clabbered milk to form a curd. Reserve whey and remove curd. Add salt to taste. Heat an iron skillet to medium hot, add curd and cook, stirring constantly with a wooden spoon. When done, the curd will become shiny and stringy and stretchy. If it dries out too much, add a little reserved whey. Break into small balls and pat and work on a table into patties like tortillas. Any juice left in the skillet can be poured over the patties to keep them moist.

The two above old recipes and information courtesy of Mary L. Williams.

BARBECUED POT ROAST

3 pound pot roast
2 teaspoons salt
1 (8 oz.) can tomato sauce
3 medium onions
2 cloves garlic
2 tablespoons brown sugar
¼ teaspoon paprika
¼ teaspoon pepper
3 tablespoons fat
½ cup water
½ teaspoon dry mustard
¼ cup catsup
¼ cup lemon juice
½ cup vinegar
1 tablespoon Worcestershire sauce
2 tablespoons flour

Rub meat with salt and pepper. Brown in hot fat. Add water, tomato sauce, minced onion and garlic. Cover and cook over low heat for 1½ hours. Combine remaining ingredients and pour over meat, cover and continue cooking for 1 hour or until tender. Remove meat to hot platter. Skim fat from gravy. Dilute with water to suit taste. Thicken with flour and serve.

Mrs. Rumaldo Segura, Not Just Another Cookbook (1983)

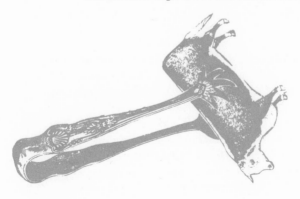

FORT SNELLING

FORT SNELLING was built in 1819-20 on a commanding bluff above the confluence of the Mississippi and Minnesota Rivers. It was the first American settlement in what is now Minnesota and the furthest outpost of the United States authority in the northwestern wilderness.

U.S. Army personnel and their families were quartered at the Fort (often two families in a single room). The Fort was a haven for explorers, French-Canadian fur trappers (who exchanged deer skins for food), and other travelers who sought safety and society within its limestone walls. Local Indians were also frequent visitors to the Fort.

The cooking at Fort Snelling included the leaden bread that was the soldiers' daily ration, French "voyageur" (trapper) cooking, and the pemmican (beef jerky) of the Indians. The recipes that follow are modern equivalents of traditional French-Canadian dishes.

TOURTIERE PIE

Pastry for 2 crusts
1½ pounds fresh pork, ground coarsely
 1 medium-sized onion, ground fine
 ¼ teaspoon allspice
 ¼ teaspoon summer savory
 ¼ teaspoon sage
 ½ teaspoon salt
 ⅛ teaspoon pepper

Mix pork, onion, and spices together and put into a pastry-lined pie tin. Top with a second crust and seal edges. Prick top crust and bake for 1 hour in a hot oven (400 degrees).

Reprinted from 100 Years of Good Cooking, *Virginia Huck, Ann H. Anderson, Eds., (Minnesota Historical Society Press, St. Paul, 1958)*

FRENCH PEA SOUP

2 quarts water
2 cups green split peas
  Cooked ham bone
2 stalks celery, chopped
2 carrots chopped
1 onion, chopped
¼ teaspoon thyme
¼ teaspoon marjoram
  Dash cayenne
1 bay leaf
  Salt and pepper to taste

Combine ingredients, cover, and boil for 20 minutes. Then reduce heat and simmer about 40 minutes longer, until peas are done. Discard ham bone. Force remaining ingredients through coarse wire strainer and serve with croutons on top. Makes 8 servings.

PIGS FEET STEW WITH DUMPLINGS

2-4 pigs feet or pork hocks
  4 celery leaves
     Salt and pepper to taste
  1 onion, chopped

Dumplings

  1 cup flour
  2 teaspoons baking powder
½ teaspoon salt
  1 teaspoon butter
¼ cup cold water

Place pigs feet in a pan with salt, pepper, celery leaves and onion. Cover with water and boil until meat is tender and separates from the bone easily. To make dumplings, sift together the flour, baking powder and salt in a mixing bowl. Rub in the butter lightly until all is well blended. Add the water and mix until the dough will hold together. Drop the dumplings by spoonfuls into the stew, cover, and allow to boil for 10 minutes. Serve hot.

FORT VANCOUVER NATIONAL HISTORIC SITE

FORT VANCOUVER IN VANCOUVER, Washington was the headquarters for the Hudson Bay Company. Established in 1825 and occupied only by the British, this trading post stocked supplies for the fur brigades and for the Indian and settler trade.

Within the walls of the Fort a strict class structure was upheld. Clerks and officers from the British Isles formed the "gentlemen" class. The lower class or "engages" made up the remaining population of the Fort.

The dining hall reflected this social distinction. The "gentlemen" met three times a day for what was called "public mess"— engages and women (even wives of gentlemen) not admitted.

The cooking, which was mostly English, was done by French Canadians over an open hearth. One of the clerks was responsible for overseeing the workings of the kitchen. The following recipes are adapted for conventional ovens, but historically roast potatoes were done in a small oven while the other recipes were and can still be made over an open hearth if cooked for the same period of time and the fire is properly regulated.

41

ENGLISH ROAST POTATOES

8-10 medium sized potatoes
      Vegetable oil

Peel potatoes and cut into half (use fewer potatoes for smaller servings). Lightly parboil potatoes for 10 minutes. After parboiling potatoes, drain well and set aside. Put ¼" to ½" oil in an approximately 14" x 8" pan (you can use a smaller pan for fewer potatoes) and pre-heat pan. Put potatoes into pan. Spoon heated oil over potatoes. Roast potatoes in a 400 degree oven for approximately 1 hour and 15 minutes or until outside of potatoes is crusty. Turn potatoes every 15 minutes.

YORKSHIRE PUDDING

½ cup drippings from prime rib roast
5 eggs
2 cups of milk
2 cups of flour
¼ teaspoon salt

Pour drippings from prime rib roast into a pan approximately 10" x 12". Beat mixture until evenly blended, but do not overbeat. Preheat pan with fat in oven. Pour mixture into pan and bake at 450 degrees about 30 minutes.

STANDING RIB ROAST

Select a 2- or 3-rib standing rib roast (4 to 5 pounds). Place fat side up in roasting pan; season with salt and pepper and place in 350 degree oven. Do not cover and do not add water.

Allow 18 to 20 minutes per pound for rare roasts, 22 to 25 minutes per pound for medium, and 27 to 30 minutes per pound for well-done roasts. Serve with Yorkshire Pudding.

ENGLISH PLUM PUDDING

    1 cup hot milk
    1 cup dry bread crumbs
 ½-¾ cup sugar
    4 egg yolks, well beaten
    ½ pound seeded raisins or currants, cut in pieces
       Flour
    ¼ pound figs, chopped
  2-3 ounces of citron, cut fine
    ½ pound of suet, chopped
    ¼ cup brandy
    1 teaspoon nutmeg
    ¾ teaspoon cinnamon
    ¼ teaspoon clove
    ¼ teaspoon mace
   1½ teaspoons salt
    4 egg whites

Pour hot milk and bread crumbs into a bowl. Add sugar, egg yolks, and raisins which have been dusted in flour. Add figs and citron. Work suet with fingers or a spoon until creamy. Add the above mixture to the suet. Stir in brandy, nutmeg, cinnamon, clove, mace and salt. Beat egg whites until stiff and fold into pudding mixture. Steam six hours. Serve pudding flaming with brandy and custard sauce.

THE GREATER YELLOWSTONE AREA

YELLOWSTONE NATIONAL PARK—the "grand old
park"—is the oldest national park in the
United States. It is situated in the Rocky
Mountains in the northwest corner of Wyoming
and extends into Montana and Idaho.

Until the late 19th Century fur trappers,
Native Americans and pioneers hunted and ate
what they found in this vast and beautiful
territory. The Plains Indian Tribes--the Sioux,
Cheyenne and Blackfoot--migrated to this area
in late summer and early fall to hunt the game
that freely roamed in abundance. Meat not
eaten or used for clothing and shelter was
preserved or dried and made into jerky. Jerky
was a staple and source of protein during the
long winter months or on the trail.

Although national park regulations
prohibit the hunting of any wildlife in the park,
moose, elk and deer are still found and
permitted to be hunted in areas outside the
park. The recipes included make use of the
meats and berries of the Northern Rockies and
give a flavor of this rugged country to the
reader.

MOOSE (OR BEEF) CHILI BAKE

1   pound lean ground moose meat or beef
1   medium onion, chopped
2   cans cream of chicken soup
     (10 ¾ oz. size)
1   tall can evaporated milk
     (13 oz. size)
1   small can evaporated milk
     (5 ⅓ oz. size)
1   can green chilis, chopped
     (4 oz.)
12   corn tortillas, 6-inch size, cut in fourths
½   pound longhorn cheese, shredded

Brown meat and onions in a heavy skillet. Mix soup, evaporated milk and chilis until smooth. Combine meat and soup mixture. Cover bottom of greased pan (9″ x 13″) with half of the tortilla quarters. Spoon half of the meat mixture over tortillas. Arrange remaining tortillas on top. Spoon on remaining meat mixture. Sprinkle top with cheese. Bake uncovered in preheated 350 degree oven about 30 minutes or until bubbly.

BERRY SOUP - A SIOUX INDIAN RECIPE

1½ pounds meat in the form of a thick steak
1 can of beef consomme
1 medium-size white onion
1 cup of fresh or frozen blackberries
½ cup of fat
1 tablespoon light honey

Broil the steak until browned on either side. Set aside to cool. Slice onions and brown them in the fat in a heavy skillet or saucepan. When meat is cool enough to touch, slice into small mouth-sized bits, and add the partially cooked meat to the onions with the blackberries. Add consomme and honey to cover the meat, and simmer until the meat is tender. If the berries are too tart, add more honey for sweetener. Salt to taste and serve.

MARINATED JERKY

5 pounds game meat or beef, cut into strips
1 part soy sauce
3 parts water
3 tablespoons salt
1 teaspoon pepper
1 teaspoon ground ginger

Place meat in a large crock, cover with soy sauce and water (1:3 mix). Add salt, pepper and ginger. Mix well, and marinate for 12 hours in refrigerator. Drain marinade and rinse the meat for 15 minutes under running water. Place meat strips on racks in oven or smokehouse and cure for 48 hours or until the desired dryness is secured.

Recipes courtesy of the Museum of the Yellowstone, West Yellowstone, Montana

Jacksonville, Oregon
Gold Rush Town

AFTER GOLD WAS DISCOVERED in Jacksonville, Oregon in 1851, thousands of gold-crazed prospectors came seeking their fortune. In their wake came wagon trains loaded with settlers and their families who formed an agricultural community.

These settlers or emigrants had to travel 2,000 back-breaking and dangerous miles from the Missouri to the Pacific, making do with limited supplies of food and cooking utensils. An emigrant guide of the period, written by Lansford Warren Hastings, recommended that each emigrant should supply himself with at least:

"two hundred pounds of flour, or meal; one hundred and fifty pounds of bacon; ten pounds of coffee; twenty pounds of sugar; and ten pounds of salt, together with such other provisions, ample as to variety. The quantity of provisions would be the same as that which would be required at home for the same length of time."

In Jacksonville's early days (in the absence of modern-day freezers) beef was stored for months in stone jars according to the following recipe:

Corned Beef and Pork Brine

To each 100 pounds of meat use: 3 pounds of sugar, brown preferred; 7 pounds of common salt; ¼ pound of baking soda. Add 4 gallons of water and bring to boil. When all is dissolved, set off to cool. Have meat cut up and packed tightly in large stone jars weighted down with cover and weight. Pour over this the cold brine. Let set for a few days. If scum forms, pour off the brine and reheat, cool and pour over the meat again. The bacon pieces may be smoked first, hams and shoulder pieces must be kept in longer. If beef is made into corned beef, it may also be kept in longer according to the size of the piece.

Grandfather Cardwell's recipe from Early Jacksonville, Oregon

CORNED BEEF

Wash the corned beef well to remove brine. If very salty, soak ½ hour in cold water; or bring to a boil, then drain. Place in large kettle, cover with boiling water, and simmer 3 hours, or until tender.

APPLE BREAD

2 cups flour, sifted
2 teaspoons baking powder
1 teaspoon salt
½ teaspoon cinnamon
¼ teaspoon nutmeg
½ cup butter
1¼ cups sugar
2 eggs
1½ cups apples, peeled and grated
½ cup walnuts, chopped

Combine first 5 ingredients and set aside. Mix butter and sugar until light and creamy. Beat in eggs one at a time, beating well after each addition. Stir in dry ingredients and apples. Mix well. Fold in nuts. Pour mixture into well greased and floured 9x5x3-inch loaf pan. Bake in moderate oven (350 degrees) for one hour or until done.

BROILED SALMON STEAKS

8 salmon steaks
Juice of 1 lemon
Flour for dredging
Salt and paprika to taste
Salad oil

Sprinkle salmon steaks generously with lemon juice. Flour only one side. Place floured side down in pre-heated broiler pan containing enough oil to cover bottom of pan. Turn immediately. Sprinkle with salt and paprika and broil until well browned without turning, or about 12 minutes. Serve with lemon or tartar sauce. Serves 8.

THE JEFFERSON MEMORIAL

THE JEFFERSON MEMORIAL BUILDING in Forest Park, St. Louis, home of the Missouri Historical Society, stands as a legacy of the St. Louis World's Fair of 1904. It is also a reminder of Thomas Jefferson's historic Louisiana Purchase, which doubled the area of the young republic and assured this nation a major role in the settlement of North America.

After acquiring this territory, Jefferson commissioned Meriwether Lewis and William Clark to explore the new land and, if possible, make their way to the Pacific Coast. They left St. Louis in May, 1804. On the trail they not only mapped out the terrain, but made zoological and botanical discoveries. The explorers frequently ate deer meat, as well as mountain ram, which they thought even more delicate than deer.

Lewis and Clark also collected seeds and plants such as wild currants, gooseberries and perhaps persimmon; these were later planted at Monticello.

The recipe for venison comes from *Thomas Jefferson's Cook Book,* while the persimmon pudding makes use of the fruit found on the trail.

Venison

*Lard well a saddle of venison, dust with salt and
pepper. Put in a hot oven. Baste with cream, as it is not
very fat. Serve with currant jelly sauce.*

Mrs. Horace Mann

PERSIMMON PUDDING

2	cups persimmon pulp
2	cups sugar
3	beaten eggs
1	teaspoon baking soda
1¼	cups buttermilk
2	cups cake flour (or 2 cups less 4 tablespoons regular flour)
1	teaspoon baking powder
½	teaspoon cinnamon
1	ounce of butter

Mix persimmon, sugar, and eggs together. Mix baking
soda with buttermilk and add to egg mixture. Add
flour, baking powder and cinnamon to batter. Melt
butter in a 13″ x 19″ x 2″ pan. Pour excess butter into
batter and stir. Pour batter into pan and bake for one
hour at 350 degrees. Cake will rise and then fall as it
cools. Cut cake into squares and serve with whipped
cream. This is a very heavy moist pudding.

From the Meriwether Lewis Collection Notebook comes a recipe for Charlotte Russe. Although it is doubtful that Lewis had the nerve to ask Sacajawea, the Indian guide, to whip eggs on the trail, the recipe does offer the reader a glimpse of the past.

Charlotte Russe

Dissolve one ounce of isinglas (gelatine) in a tumbler of water, add to it three tumblers of new milk and one large vanilla bean bruised, boil it slowly until reduced to one third, beat the yolk of 6 eggs with 8 ounces of fine sugar. Pour the infusion upon the eggs and sugar, stir it well and return it to the sauce pan, place it on the fire again, stirring it until it begins to thicken; as you are about to take it off the fire stir in the white of the eggs. Sit it away to cool and when perfectly cold, have a pint of thick sweet cream beaten to a froth, add this to the mixture. Pour it into a form surrounded by ginger or sugar cake, set on ice or in some cold place where it must remain an hour before you turn it out of the mould.

 ## RASPBERRY CHARLOTTE RUSSE

 2 tablespoons gelatin
½ cup cold water
 1 pint heavy cream
¼ cup confectioners' sugar
 1 package frozen raspberries, thawed
12 lady fingers

Soak gelatin in water 5 minutes, place over hot water and stir until dissolved. Beat the cream until very stiff; gradually add sugar, the dissolved gelatin and the syrup from the raspberries, beating all the time. When the mixture begins to thicken stir in the raspberries. Pour into a mold lined with split lady fingers, and chill until firm.

MESA VERDE NATIONAL PARK

MESA VERDE NATIONAL PARK, located in the
high plateau country of southwestern
Colorado, contains remarkable cliff dwellings
which are the remains of an ancient culture
known as Anasazi.

The Anasazi, (a Navajo word meaning
"ancient ones") occupied Mesa Verde (Spanish
for "green table") for over 700 years. They
built elaborate stone cities, which still exist
today, in the recesses of the canyon walls.

Although the Anasazi were an agricultural
people, they had constant problems in both
farming and seeking out other food sources.
They grew crops such as corn, beans and
squash on the mesa tops. They also gathered
plants like pinyon nuts and juniper berries and
hunted for deer, rabbit and squirrels. Their
only domestic animals were dogs and turkeys.

At the first World Conference on Cultural
Parks at Mesa Verde a reception was held
which featured foods indigenous to the area
that may have been eaten by the Anasazi. Just
turn the page to savor the menu from this
reception together with recipes utilizing food
available to the Anasazi, adapted for modern-
day preparation.

Menu From World Conference On Cultural Parks Dinner

Brochette of Rabbit, Mushrooms and Squash with
Gooseberry Glaze
Brochette of Duck and Mushrooms with Choke Cherry
Glaze
Galantine of Turkey with Juniper Berry Sauce
Escabeche of Brook Trout
Rabbit Pate
American Salmon Caviar on Corn Blinis
Roast Top Round of Elk
Roast Barron of Bison
Whole Poached Salmon with Prickly Pear Sauce
Smoked Breast of Turkey with Hot Plum Preserves
Corn Bread Sticks
Mushrooms filled with Turkey and Pinyon Nuts
Mushrooms filled with Forced Meat of Venison and
Fresh Coriander
Roast Goose with Apples and Walnuts
Honey Cakes
Apple Tarts
Prickly Pear Tarts
Pumpkin Pie
Squash and Pinyon Nut Cake
Goat Cheese
Fresh Strawberries
Clover Honey

Wild Turkey Roast

1   8-pound wild turkey (domestic fowl may be used)
    Salt and pepper to taste
1   cup melted butter

Dress and clean turkey. Rub inside and out with salt
and pepper. Stuff cavity loosely with stuffing. Fasten
opening with metal pins. Brush with half of melted
butter. Roast at 350 degrees for 3 to 4 hours basting
with butter every half hour.

PINYON NUT STUFFING

4   cups bread crumbs
2   cups pinyon nuts, shelled and roasted
1   medium onion, chopped
½   cup mushrooms, sliced
1   egg, beaten
⅓   cup melted butter
1   teaspoon salt
½   teaspoon pepper
½   teaspoon wild sage, crumbled

Melt shortening in skillet, add onion and mushrooms and saute 5 minutes. Add crumbs, seasonings, egg and pinyon nuts. Toss to mix thoroughly. Fill cavity of turkey with stuffing.

REFRIED PINTO BEANS

2   cups pinto beans, cooked
2   tablespoons bacon fat
4   tablespoons onion, minced
4   tablespoons Cheddar cheese, grated

Saute onion in bacon fat. Mash the cold cooked beans and add to onions stirring constantly until completely dry. Add cheese while cooking the beans slowly.

MOUNT RUSHMORE
NATIONAL MEMORIAL

THE HEADS OF FOUR AMERICAN PRESIDENTS have been carved in bold relief on the granite face of Mount Rushmore, in the Black Hills of South Dakota.

Each of these presidents made a unique contribution to the United States. George Washington led his nation in its struggle for independence. Thomas Jefferson created a representative government. Abraham Lincoln established a permanent Union of the states and promoted equality of all people. Theodore Roosevelt helped the United States to emerge as a central figure in world affairs.

Just as these presidents each made his own mark on history, they differed in their attitudes concerning food. While Washington enjoyed and partook of good food, it was Martha Washington who supervised and was responsible for the gracious and elegant dinners served in New York and Mount Vernon. Conversely, Thomas Jefferson was intimately concerned with all aspects of the food he ate from the importing and growing of seeds to the preparation of foods and the recording of recipes.

While Jefferson was a true connoisseur of the domestic arts, Lincoln could go days without eating. His law partner William H. Herndon once said, "Abe can sit and think longer without food than any man I ever met." On the other hand, Theodore Roosevelt by his own admission liked, "coarse food and plenty of it."

Martha Washington's Great Cake

To make a great Cake

Take 40 eggs and divide the whites from the yolks & beat them to a froth then work 4 pounds of butter to a cream & put the whites of eggs to it a Spoon full at a time till it is well work'd then put 4 pounds of sugar finely powdered to it in the same manner then put in the Youlks of eggs & 5 pounds of flower & 5 pounds of fruit. 2 hours will bake it add to it half an ounce of mace & nutmeg half a pint of wine & some frensh brandy.

Transcribed from the original manuscript in the collections of the Mount Vernon Ladies' Association.

FRUIT CAKE

½ pound candied cherries	½ cup sugar
¼ pound walnut meats	½ cup honey
¼ pound pecan meats	5 eggs, well beaten
½ pound pitted dates	1½ cups flour
¼ pound preserved citron	1 teaspoon salt
½ pound seeded raisins	1 teaspoon baking powder
¼ pound lemon peel	1 teaspoon allspice
¼ pound orange peel	½ teaspoon nutmeg
¼ cup flour	½ teaspoon mace
1 cup flour	½ teaspoon cloves
1 cup butter	¼ cup orange juice

Cut up fruit peels; halve cherries, nut meats, and dates; cut citron the size of almonds. Dredge fruits in ¼ cup flour.Cream shortening and sugar; add honey, then eggs, and beat well. Add flour sifted with dry ingredients alternately with fruit juice; beat thoroughly. Pour batter over floured fruits and mix well. Line greased 3½ x 7½-inch loaf pans with waxed paper, allowing ½ inch to extend above all sides of pan. Pour batter into pans; do not flatten.

Bake in 250 degree oven 3 to 4 hours. Place can containing 2 cups water on bottom shelf of oven while baking.

If decoration of almonds and cherries is used, place on cakes at end of 2 hours. If desired, pour brandy over cake and wrap in a brandy-soaked cloth. Store in a covered container in a cool place.

THEODORE ROOSEVELT'S EGGPLANT-AND-TOMATO CASSEROLE

1   eggplant
½   cup butter or margarine
1   small onion
4   tomatoes
2   teaspoons salt
    Dash pepper
1   tablespoon brown sugar
¼   cup dry bread crumbs
¼   cup grated Parmesan cheese

Heat your oven to 375 degrees. Wash eggplant and cut into ½ inch slices (don't bother peeling). Fry in melted butter or margarine until lightly browned on both sides but not wholly cooked (takes 2 to 3 minutes). Transfer slices to a plate for the moment. Now chop onion fine and fry in the eggplant skillet until limp. Cut tomatoes in chunks, toss in with onions along with salt, pepper, sugar and cook gently for 5 to 7 minutes. Arrange a layer of eggplant slices on the bottom of a 2-quart casserole or baking dish, spoon all the tomatoes on top, add another layer of eggplant and top with a mixture of bread crumbs and Parmesan cheese. Bake 20 to 30 minutes or until top of the casserole is nicely browned. Serves 6.

Jefferson's Snow Eggs

Take 10 eggs; separate the yolks from the whites and beat the whites as you do for Savoy cake, till you can turn the vessel bottom upward without their leaving it; when they are well beaten put in 2 spoonfuls of powdered sugar & a little orange flower water or rose water if you prefer it. Put a pint of milk in a saucepan with 6 oz. sugar and orange flower or rose water; when your milk boils take the whites, spoonful by spoonful & do them in the boiling milk; when sufficiently poached, take them out & lay them on a sieve; take out a part of the milk, according to the thickness you wish to give the custard, beat up the yolks & stir them in the remainder; as soon as it thickens take the mixture from the fire, strain it through a sieve; dish up your whites & pour the custard over them.

A little wine stirred in is a great improvement.

James, cook at Monticello

SNOW EGGS

4 cups milk
3 eggs, separated
½ cup sugar
½ teaspoon salt
½ teaspoon vanilla
1 tablespoon cornstarch

Heat the milk. Mix sugar, salt, and cornstarch; add to slightly beaten yolks and 1 white of egg. Pour the hot milk on the beaten yolks. Cook this mixture in a double boiler until it thickens, stirring constantly. When cool, stir in flavoring. Beat the 2 whites until stiff, fold in 2 tablespoons sugar, and drop by spoonfuls on top of cold custard.

LINCOLN'S VANILLA PECAN PIE

3 eggs beaten
½ cup dark brown sugar
1 cup light corn syrup
3 tablespoons butter
1½ teaspoons vanilla
⅛ teaspoon salt

1 cup chopped pecans
1 tablespoon flour
1 9″ pie shell
Whip cream garnish
Pecan halves

Preheat oven to 375 degrees. Combine eggs and brown sugar, blend in corn syrup, melt butter and add along with vanilla and salt. Blend pecans with flour and add to mixture. Pour in 9″ crust. Bake at 375 degrees for 40 minutes or until firm. Garnish with whipped cream. Makes 8 servings.

THEODORE ROOSEVELT'S CHICKEN FRICASSE, CREOLE STYLE

4 to 5 pound chicken
fresh or frozen
¼ cup butter, margarine
or shortening
¼ cup flour
2 cups water

1 medium onion
6 fresh tomatoes
Few sprigs parsley, chopped
1 tablespoon salt
Dash of pepper

Cut chicken into serving pieces. Melt fat in a heavy frying pan, add chicken pieces and brown slowly on all sides. Now lift out chicken and transfer to a heavy kettle or saucepan—one with a tightly fitting cover. Add flour to the chicken drippings stirring constantly until smooth. Add water gradually and stir until gravy bubbles. Pour over chicken, toss in chopped onion, peeled tomatoes, fresh parsley, salt and pepper. Cover tightly and cook over a low heat for 1¼ to 1½ hours or until chicken is very tender. Serves 4 to 6. Delicious with steamed rice.

PALACE OF THE GOVERNORS

THE PALACE OF THE GOVERNORS in Santa Fe, New Mexico is the oldest public building in the United States. Today the building contains the history division of the Museum of New Mexico.

The Palace was in turn controlled by the Spanish, Indians, Mexicans and Americans; and it is thus not surprising that the cooking of New Mexico incorporates elements from all four cultures. It is this blend of cultures that makes New Mexican food unique and delicious.

The Palace was built in 1610 by the Spanish Governor Pedro de Peralta. It was never a beautiful place. Dirt floors, small unglazed windows and adobe walls are not most people's notion of a palace.

For over 250 years, except for the years 1680-1692 when the Pueblo Indians took control of the Palace, the building contained the residences and offices of the governors of New Mexico under the regimes of Spain, Mexico and the United States.

The recipes for sopaipillas, picante sauce, flan and guacamole give a taste of the cuisine that sustained various occupants of the Palace.

Sopaipillas

- 4 cups flour
- 1 teaspoon salt
- 1¾ cups lukewarm water
- 3 teaspoons baking powder
- ¼ cup sugar

Combine all ingredients to form a sticky dough. Put a quarter of the dough onto a floured board and knead until smooth and not sticky. Pat it into a rectangle about ¼ inch thick. Cut into diamond shapes and cut 2 slashes into each piece, so that when it is fried it looks somewhat like a pretzel. Deepfry on both sides until golden. Dip into honey, or a mixture of corn syrup and melted butter.

Mary E. Larson Smith

Picante Sauce

- 1 can tomato sauce
- 1 large fresh tomato, diced
- ½ teaspoon dried taco sauce mix
- 1 small can diced green chilis
- 1 can Spanish-style tomato sauce
- 1 bunch green onions, chopped
- ½ teaspoon or more crushed dried red peppers

Combine all ingredients and serve with tortilla or corn chips.

Agnes Soliz

FLAN

6   egg yolks
¼   cup sugar
1   cup milk
1   cup light cream
¾   teaspoon vanilla
⅛   teaspoon salt

Beat egg yolks, then stir in the rest of the ingredients. Put 6 custard bowls in a baking dish whose sides are higher than the bowls, then pour boiling water into the pan until the water level almost reaches the sides of the bowls. Pour custard mixture into bowls, and bake at 350 degrees for about half an hour, or until a knife inserted into the custard comes out clean. Serve either hot or cold.

GUACAMOLE

2   avocados
1   chopped tomato
½   minced onion
1   tablespoon lime or lemon juice
¼   teaspoon garlic salt
    Salt and pepper

If the avocados are hard when you buy them in the store, allow them to ripen (not in the refrigerator!) until they begin to feel a little bit soft to the touch. Cut them in half, remove stones, and mash up the avocado meat with the rest of the ingredients. Use as a party dip with corn chips or tortilla chips, or use as a garnish on any salad. Dabs of guacamole may be topped with a teaspoonful of sour cream sprinkled with paprika for added decoration.

Saguaro National Monument

IN Saguaro National Monument in Tucson, Arizona, the saguaro (Sa-WAR-O) cactus, the symbol of the American West, stands tall among many other desert plants in the Sonoran Desert.

To the Papago Indians, whose homeland has always been in the Sonoran Desert, the saguaro is an Indian; to harm it is to harm one's brother or sister.

During the month of June thousands of tiny seeds inside the rosy ripe fruit of the saguaro are scattered on the ground. The Papago would gather great quantities of fruit by knocking the fruit pods down with poles, and eating them like candy or making wine from the fruit for their rain ceremonies.

Many foods can be made from the variety of plants found in the desert. One is a fine jelly made from the Engelman's prickly pear cactus; another is hackberry jam made from the desert hackberry, a low tree found in the Sonoran Desert. The bark from the mesquite tree can be used as cooking fuel, and lends the taste and aroma of the Southwestern desert to meats cooked over its coals.

Prickly Pear Jelly

1   quart of prickly pear fruit
1¾ ounce package of powdered pectin
3   tablespoons lemon or lime juice
3½ cups sugar

Gather a quart of fruit to make 2½ cups of juice. Do not use over-ripe fruit. Use kitchen tongs or fork to sever fruit from plant. Using a candle hold fruit with tongs and burn off spines, being careful not to get them in fingers. Rinse and place fruit in a kettle with enough water to cover fruit. Boil until tender, about one hour. Press with potato masher to break skins, then strain through a jelly bag or two thicknesses of cheese cloth. Add pectin to 2½ cups of juice and bring to a fast boil stirring constantly. Add lemon or lime juice and sugar. Bring to a hard boil stirring constantly. Remove from fire, skim and pour into sterilized jelly glasses.

Papago Hackberry Jam

1½ cups desert hackberries
1   tablespoon lemon juice
½   cup white sugar
2   tablespoons water

Combine ingredients in heavy saucepan. Mash berries with potato masher to release some juice. Bring to boil, then reduce heat so mixture is simmering. Stir often to prevent sticking and burning. Cook and stir for 10 minutes until mixture has boiled down and is quite thick. Syrup will thicken as it cools.

MESQUITE STEAK

Mesquite chips
Charcoal
Sirloin steak

Cover mesquite chips with water and soak for two hours. Then combine charcoal and mesquite in your outdoor grill, using three parts charcoal to one part mesquite chips. Light fire and cook steak in usual fashion. (Lamb chops, hamburgers, chicken or fish can also be grilled mesquite-style.)

SAN FRANCISCO CHINATOWN

MANY CHINESE FROM CANTON, lured by the California gold rush, emigrated to the United States around 1850. A large portion settled in San Francisco, which they called gum shan or the "Gold Mountain."

The Chinese were excluded from all but the most menial jobs. The ideal solution to this problem was self-employment; with very little capital a Chinese could open a laundry or restaurant.

The first Chinese restaurants were modest affairs with limited menus. One dish that was often served was chop suey, meaning miscellaneous fragments. Chop suey was an American invention, although based on Chinese mixtures. It was inexpensive to produce and delighted the white miners whose meals were otherwise far from exciting.

Another standby of Chinese restaurants was chow mein. This dish originated in China where it was (and is) often eaten as a snack or light meal.

The modern recipes which follow probably approximate Chinese cooking in California in the 19th Century and certainly allow the reader a gastronomic stroll through San Francisco's Chinatown.

CHOP SUEY

1 pound beef tenderloin, cut into thin strips
2 tablespoons oil
1 large onion, sliced
1 clove garlic, chopped fine
3 stalks celery, diagonally chopped
12 water chestnuts
½ pound pea sprouts
12 mushrooms, sliced
¼ cup water

Thickening

1 teaspoon soy sauce
1 teaspoon cornstarch
1 teaspoon salt
½ teaspoon sugar
¼ cup water

Fry beef in oil over high heat for 3 minutes, stirring constantly. Remove beef from pan. Fry onion and garlic. Add vegetables, except pea sprouts, and water. Cover and cook for 5 minutes. Add cooked beef and pea sprouts and mix thoroughly with vegetables for 2 minutes. Just before serving, add thickening which has been mixed together ahead of time. Stir constantly until sauce has thickened. Serve immediately with hot rice.

ALMOND CHOW MEIN

1	pound noodles
	Oil for deep frying
¼	pound mushrooms
¼	pound bamboo shoots
¼	pound water chestnuts
⅛	cup chicken meat, cooked and thinly sliced
⅛	cup cooked ham, thinly sliced
	Salt, pepper, soy sauce and ginger to taste
2	eggs
½	cup almonds, roasted

Cook noodles in salted, boiling water for 5 minutes. Drain and run cold water over them. Dry noodles for ½ hour and drop into deep fat. Remove from pot quickly and drain fat off on brown paper. Fry mushrooms, bamboo shoots, and water chestnuts in a greased frying pan or wok until tender, and then season with salt, pepper, soybean sauce and ginger to taste. Remove vegetables from pan, and fry noodles. Next, place a layer of noodles, a layer of vegetables, and a layer of chicken and ham on a large platter. Beat 2 eggs and fry in a greased pan. Slice very fine and spread on top of chicken and ham. Sprinkle almonds over the chow mein, and trim with parsley if desired.

THE SANTA BARBARA MISSION

THE FRANCISCAN FATHERS between 1769 and 1823 established 21 missions in California on El Camino Real. The Santa Barbara Mission, the "Queen" of the missions, was founded in 1786 by Fr. Fermin Lasuen and is the only mission never abandoned by the Franciscans and still in use today.

The Fathers educated the local Chumash Indians in Christian doctrine. They also taught the Indians, who were pre-agricultural, how to farm and raise cattle, and as a result the Mission soon became self-supporting. The Indians, who had previously lived on fish from the Pacific Ocean, on seeds and on wild animals, planted and harvested wheat, maize, barley, beans and chick peas. Food was prepared by Indian women under the direction of the Fathers.

Indian maize or field corn was made into nixtamal, a hominy corn, and immediately ground into masa, the original base for tortillas and other early Mexican, Spanish and mission dishes. Atole, a porridge made with masa, was eaten by the Indians at any meal. Recipes for atole and other mission foods are included in the following pages.

Atole

1   cup masa
2   cups cold water
½   teaspoon salt
2   cups milk
    Sugar to taste

Mix the masa with water and salt. In a double boiler
boil mixture until thick. Add the milk and sugar to
taste and simmer, stirring constantly until thickened.
Serve hot with additional sugar or fruit if desired.
Serves 6-8.

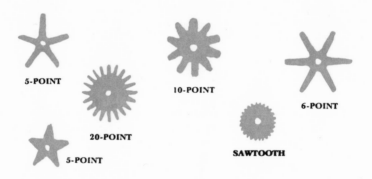

5-POINT

20-POINT

10-POINT

6-POINT

5-POINT

SAWTOOTH

Roast Corn, Garlic Buttered

Remove outer husks and loosen inner husks,
removing silk carefully; trim ear if necessary. Brush
kernels generously with garlic butter. Tie inner husks
into their original position, and lay on grill above
glowing coals. Turn frequently. Ten to 25 minutes will
be required to roast corn.

To make "garlic butter" slice 3 cloves of garlic and
add to ¼ pound of soft butter. Mix well and let stand
at room temperature, stirring occasionally.

Fried Abalone

8   slices abalone
    Salt and pepper to taste
2   eggs beaten
    Bread crumbs
    Butter
4   tablespoons lemon juice
2   tablespoons Nasturtium seeds or capers

Pound slices of abalone vigorously with a wooden mallet. Wipe dry, sprinkle with salt and pepper, dip into well-beaten egg and then into bread crumbs. Brown quickly in butter allowing not more than 1½ to 2 minutes on each side. Combine lemon juice and seeds, or capers, and pour over abalone. Serves 8.

SITKA NATIONAL HISTORICAL PARK

SITKA NATIONAL HISTORICAL PARK is the site of the battle of 1804 that marked the last major resistance of the Tlingit Indians to Russian colonization. Sitka, in southeast Alaska, the capital of Russian America for many years, served as the center of the Russian American Company's fur and other trading operations. It was here in 1867 that the transfer of Alaska to the United States, for the sum of $7.2 million, took place. Many families with Russian ties remained in Sitka, perpetuating Russian customs and foods that still exist today.

In a Russian Orthodox home Easter surpasses Christmas in importance. Paskha, which means "Easter," is a pudding served at this time of year in addition to Kulich, a bread, which is a must on any Russian dining table. Kulich is eaten after the Easter midnight service and for three days following. Colored eggs, herring, Borscht, meats and of course Russian tea (served from a samovar into glasses, not cups, with a touch of rum) make the feast complete.

HOT RUSSIAN BORSCHT

2 pounds soup meat	1 head cabbage
1 bunch beets	2 cans tomato essence
2 carrots	1 teaspoon sauer salt
2 onions	1 teaspoon salt
3 stalks celery	2 tablespoons sugar
1 green pepper	1 cup sour cream

Boil enough water to more than cover meat. Add meat, saving cabbage until later. Add at once 1 teaspoon sauer salt, 1 teaspoon table salt, 2 tablespoons sugar. Boil 10 minutes, add tomato essence, continue boiling. Cut up cabbage and add to mixture. Turn down heat and allow to boil gently for 3 hours. During cooking, remove fat as it comes to the surface. Serve with sour cream. The boiled meat is excellent served with horseradish. Serves 6-8.

RUSSIAN TEA

1 heaping tablespoon black tea
  Pinch of cloves
6 cups freshly boiled water
4 teaspoons rum (optional)

Put tea and cloves into a small teapot which has been pre-heated. Add 1 cup water and let stand for 5 minutes. Pour a little into each glass, according to the strength desired and fill glass with additional boiling water. Add 1 teaspoon rum to each glass if desired. Yield: 4 servings.

KULICH
(Easter Bread)

2½ cups milk
⅓ cup butter
¾ cup sugar
½ teaspoon salt
1 package dry yeast
   or 1 yeast cake
8 cups flour
3 egg yolks, beaten
2 whole eggs, beaten

1 teaspoon vanilla
   or lemon extract
   or 3 drops oil of roses
1 cup raisins
1 cup candied fruit
1 cup citron
1½ cups chopped almonds
2 cups powdered sugar
1 teaspoon vanilla
   Milk or cream

Warm the milk and add butter to melt it. Add the sugar and salt and cool until tepid. Add yeast and allow to dissolve. Slowly stir in 4 cups flour. Put in warm place, raise until double in bulk. Then add the beaten egg yolks, eggs and preferred flavoring. Mix the raisins, candied fruit, citron and almonds and the remaining flour and add to dough. Knead thoroughly and raise to double bulk.

When raised, shape to fit well greased cans (1 or 2 pound coffee cans are a good size). Fill cans two-thirds full and allow to rise in a warm place until dough is over rim of can. Bake in a moderate oven (350 degrees) for 45 to 60 minutes depending on size of loaf.

When baked, remove from container and allow to cool a little. While still warm, cover top with icing made from powdered sugar, vanilla and sufficient milk or cream to make it thin enough to run down the sides of the loaf. Decorate with small colored candies. Yield: 3 to 4 loaves.

From Famous Russian Recipes, *translated by Sasha Kashevaroff, Old Harbor Press, Sitka, Alaska.*

SUTTER'S FORT

SUTTER'S FORT was established in 1839 by
John Augustus Sutter, who had come to
California from Switzerland to make his fortune
in the New World. He named his settlement
New Helvetia, or "New Switzerland," in the
area now called Sacramento.

Sutter's Fort became the first non-Indian
settlement in California's Great Central Valley.
A Mexican land grant gave Sutter over 48,000
acres of land, and in a short time, with the
help of a dozen settlers and Indian labor, he
cultivated the land, established a fur trading
post and built a brandy distillery.

In 1848 gold was discovered at John
Sutter's sawmill. Word spread quickly that
there was "gold in them thar hills" and the fort
became a wayside station for gold seekers
traveling to nearby diggings in the Mother
Lode.

Sutter never prospered from the find. He
was swindled out of his land and holdings, and
by 1849 no longer owned the fort.

The recipes that follow are Californio
dishes served in this area in the 19th Century
and adapted for today's kitchens.

CARNE OJA (BEEF COOKED IN A POT)

1 plate of beef ribs, split lengthwise (ask your butcher)
1 large onion
2 8-ounce cans of garbanzo beans
1 head of green cabbage
3 carrots
1 teaspoon whole allspice
4 cloves of garlic, chopped

1 chili pepper, a small jalepeno or larger red chili
½ teaspoon whole cloves
1 tablespoon salt
1 teaspoon fresh-ground pepper or 1 tablespoon whole peppercorns
A few sprigs of fresh cilantro
1 tablespoon dried oregano

Slice carrots into chunks and quarter the onion. Put the beef, onion, carrots, garlic, chili, herbs and spices into a pot, add water to half-cover contents, cover, and simmer for one hour. Add the garbanzos, top off with more water if necessary, cover, and simmer for another ½ hour. Quarter cabbage and place on top of meat; cook an additional 20 minutes, or until cabbage is just tender. Serves 6 generously. (Leftover broth makes delicious soup.)

BEEF A LA MODE

1	3-to 4-pound beef roast	1	bay leaf
5 or 6	mushrooms, sliced	2	teaspoons salt
1	onion	1	teaspoon pepper
½	teaspoon nutmeg	1	bottle red wine
1	teaspoon whole allspice	2	tablespoons flour
¼	teaspoon cloves	¼	cup water

Cut the onion into slices. Cut a large central pocket in the beef roast and stuff with sliced onion, mushrooms, and nutmeg. Tie the stuffed roast closed and put in cooking pot. Add any remaining mushrooms or onion. Add spices, salt and pepper, and red wine to cover. Stew slowly over low heat for 3 hours, letting wine mixture reduce with cooking. Remove and slice. Mix flour with ¼ cup water until smooth; add to hot sauce to make gravy. Pour over the sliced beef roast and serve.

Leafy Green Salad

Salad greens: spinach, endive, mustard greens, miner's lettuce, turnip greens, cut cabbage, beet leaves, etc., torn into bite-size pieces, ¼ cup oil, cured olives, pitted and chopped.

Dressing:

2 hard-boiled egg yolks (use whites for garnish)
2 teaspoons light cream
2 tablespoons olive oil
4 tablespoons vinegar
1 teaspoon stone-ground mustard

Mash the eggs yolks with cream until lumps disappear. Add mustard and mix thoroughly. Slowly beat in the oil, forming a thin paste. Whisk in the vinegar, beating rapidly. Thoroughly mix greens and olives, then toss with dressing and serve.

Index